EMOTIONS and FEELINGS

Grief

Sarah Harvey

Explore other books at:
WWW.ENGAGEBOOKS.COM

VANCOUVER, B.C.

WWW.ENGAGEBOOKS.COM

Grief: Level 2
Emotions and Feelings
Harvey, Sarah 1950 –
Text © 2023 Engage Books
Design © 2023 Engage Books

Edited by: A.R. Roumanis, Ashley Lee,
Melody Sun, and Sarah Harvey
Design by: Mandy Christiansen

Text set in Arial Regular.
Chapter headings set in PeachyKeenJF.

FIRST EDITION / FIRST PRINTING

LIBRARY AND ARCHIVES CANADA CATALOGUING IN PUBLICATION

Title: Grief / Sarah Harvey.
Names: Harvey, Sarah N., 1950- author.
Description: Series statement: Emotions and feelings

Identifiers: Canadiana (print) 20230447295 | Canadiana (ebook) 20230447309
ISBN 978-1-77878-140-7 (hardcover)
ISBN 978-1-77878-141-4 (softcover)
ISBN 978-1-77878-142-1 (epub)
ISBN 978-1-77878-143-8 (pdf)
ISBN 978-1-77878-144-5 (audio)

Subjects:
LCSH: Grief—Juvenile literature.
LCSH: Grief in children—Juvenile literature.

Classification: LCC BF723.G75 H37 2023 | DDC J155.9/37—DC23

This project has been made possible in part
by the Government of Canada.

Canada

Contents

What Is Grief?

Grief is a **complex** and strong emotion. It is a normal and natural response to loss. It is not an illness or a mental health problem.

KEY WORD

Complex: made up of many parts.

Grief is made up of emotions such as anger, fear, sadness, loneliness, and confusion. Feelings of grief may not happen for weeks, months, or even years after a loss happens.

Why Do People Grieve?

Most people **grieve** after the death of a loved one. But any loss can cause grief. A lot of small losses may cause as much grief as a single big loss.

KEY WORD

Grieve: feel grief.

You may grieve when a friend moves away or you lose a favorite toy. Losing a pet is a big loss that can be hard to deal with.

Some people may know a loved one is going to die and will grieve before their death.

Are There Different Kinds of Grief?

Grief hurts. Over time, most people are able to accept their loss. They can move forward with their lives. This is called **uncomplicated** or simple grief.

KEY WORD

Uncomplicated: not difficult or hard to understand.

Complicated grief is strong emotional pain that lasts a long time. It gets in the way of daily life. Someone feeling complicated grief has a hard time accepting their loss.

How Does Grief Affect the Way You Think?

Grief makes it hard to pay attention. It can be hard to finish tasks. You might start a book but never finish it.

Grief does not erase your memories of a loved one. They will always be there.

Misplace: put something in the wrong place and forget where it is.

Grief can also make you forget things. You may forget plans you made or **misplace** things. You may find it hard to make choices as well.

How Does Grief Affect the Way You Act?

Every person acts differently when they are grieving. Some people may not appear to act differently at all. Others may get angry easily or cry often.

Grief can make you want to run away and hide. Some people will stay in bed all day. They may not want to go out.

Can Grief Be a Good Thing?

Grief can make people want to help others. Some people start support groups for others who are grieving.

There are many online support groups that help connect people who are grieving.

Many people feel grief about the plants and animals that are dying all over the world. Their grief is leading them to help save the planet.

The World Wildlife Fund has over 11 million members. They are fighting to keep animals alive.

Does Everyone Feel Grief?

Everyone feels grief at some point in their life. Each person grieves in their own way. Some people will want to talk about how they feel. Others will not.

There is no right or wrong way to grieve. There is no timeline or roadmap. Many people still find moments of happiness when they are grieving.

What Does Grief Feel Like?

Grief feels different for everyone. Someone may get headaches or be tired all the time. They may not want to eat, or they may have a hard time sleeping.

Some people may feel worse than others when grieving.

Not feeling anything is called being numb.

Some people may not feel anything after a loss. This is okay. Do not try to force yourself to feel something.

19

Can You Stop Feeling Grief?

Some people try to shut down or avoid their feelings of grief. It might make them feel better for a little while. It is not a healthy way to deal with grief.

Shutting down your feelings makes grief last longer. It can lead to mental health problems. It can also make you feel ill.

Does Grief Ever Go Away?

Grief never fully goes away. It is normal to move in and out of grief. As time goes by, feelings of grief will not be as strong, will not last as long, and will happen less often.

You can think of grief like waves in an ocean. At first, big waves of grief knock you down. They come one right after the other. After a while, the waves start to get smaller and farther apart.

You can share stories, photos, or videos to help you remember someone you have lost.

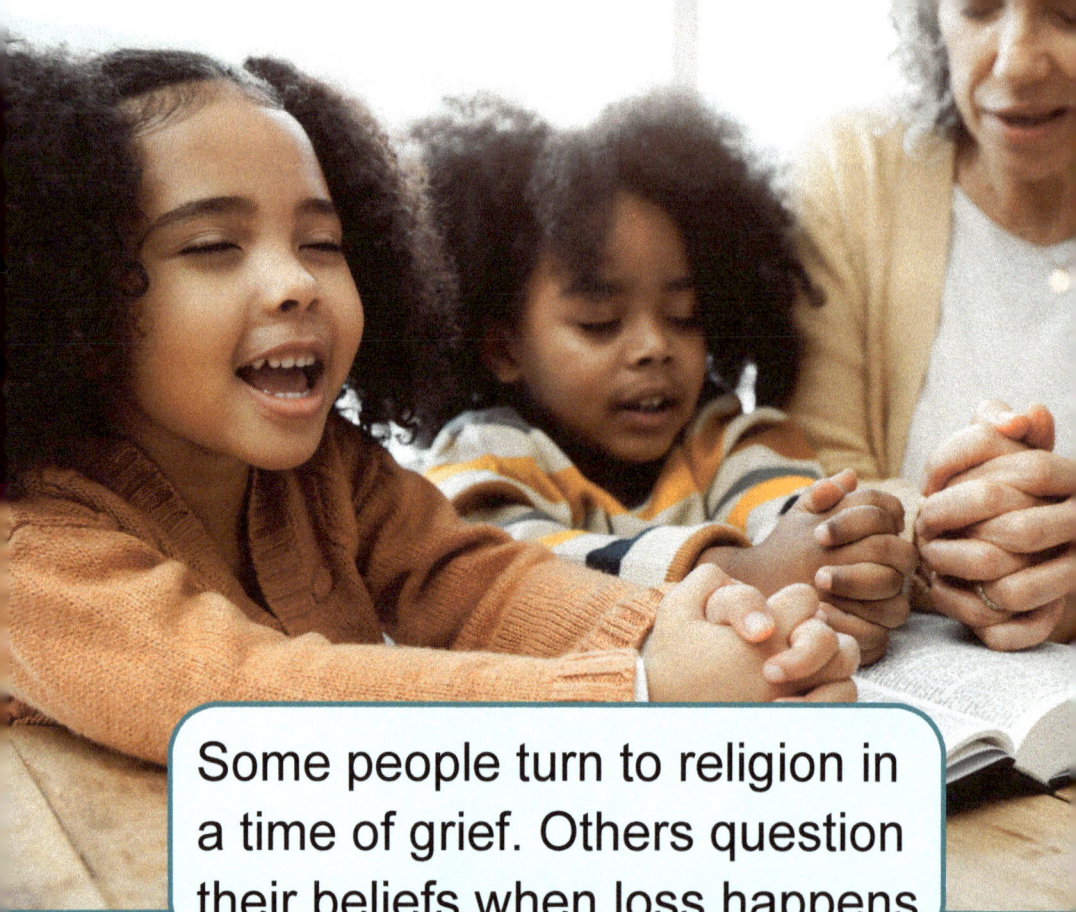

Some people turn to religion in a time of grief. Others question their beliefs when loss happens.

Does Grief Change as You Grow Older?

As you grow, you learn about the world and about yourself. This helps you understand what grief is. It does not make grief go away.

People who have lived a long time can feel a lot of grief. Many of their loved ones may have died. Some older people may grieve the loss of their health.

What Can You Do if You Are Grieving?

If your feelings become too much to handle, talk to an adult. Talking about your feelings can help you understand them.

Take care of yourself. Get lots of sleep, eat healthy foods, and get some exercise if you can. These things can help your body heal and make you feel better.

What Can You Do if Other People Are Grieving?

Do not try to make a grieving person talk. If they do want to talk, listen. Let them know you are there to **support** them.

KEY WORD

Support: help or encourage someone.

Be patient. Healing from grief can take a long time. Do not push anyone to get over it. You cannot fix it.

Quiz

Test your knowledge of grief by answering the following questions. The questions are based on what you have read in this book. The answers are listed on the bottom of the next page.

1 Is grief a mental health problem?

2 What is complicated grief?

3 Does grief erase the memories of a loved one?

4 What is it called when you do not feel anything?

5 What makes grief last longer?

6 Should you try to make a grieving person talk?

Explore other books in the Emotions and Feelings series.

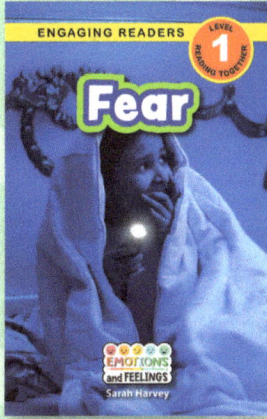

ENGAGING READERS — LEVEL 1 — READING TOGETHER
Anger
EMOTIONS and FEELINGS
Kari Jones

ENGAGING READERS — LEVEL 1 — READING TOGETHER
Fear
EMOTIONS and FEELINGS
Sarah Harvey

ENGAGING READERS — LEVEL 1 — READING TOGETHER
Happiness
EMOTIONS and FEELINGS
Kari Jones

ENGAGING READERS — LEVEL 1 — READING TOGETHER
Sadness
EMOTIONS and FEELINGS
Sarah Harvey

ENGAGING READERS — LEVEL 1 — READING TOGETHER
Surprise
EMOTIONS and FEELINGS
Kari Jones

ENGAGING READERS — LEVEL 2 — READING WITH HELP
Gratitude
EMOTIONS and FEELINGS
Kari Jones

ENGAGING READERS — LEVEL 2 — READING WITH HELP
Guilt
EMOTIONS and FEELINGS
Sarah Harvey

ENGAGING READERS — LEVEL 2 — READING WITH HELP
Love
EMOTIONS and FEELINGS
Sarah Harvey

ENGAGING READERS — LEVEL 2 — READING WITH HELP
Worry
EMOTIONS and FEELINGS
Sarah Harvey

Visit www.engagebooks.com/readers

Answers: 1. No 2. Strong emotional pain that lasts a long time 3. No 4. Being numb 5. Shutting down your feelings 6. No

31